Hacking

Full Hacking Guide for Beginners with 30
Useful Tips, All You Need To Know About
Basic Security

Table of contents

Introduction

A hacker is a clever programmer who comes up with clever solutions—"good hacks"— for computer and information security. Ethical hacking or penetration testing refers to the practice of legally hacking a system with the objective of exposing its potential vulnerabilities to malicious hacker activities. In ethical hacking, a security professional applies his hacking skills to defend information systems against those attacks orchestrated by "black hat" hackers.

To achieve useable results that are equally legal, an ethical hacker must abide by certain hard-and-fast, scientific rules. This scientific process involves a series of phases, including planning, enumeration, vulnerability analysis, exploitation, and of course, integration. A hacker should at all times during this process have a goal and plan.

The entire process should however be done ethically and with no intent to harm. A professional will always seek permission prior to his exploitations, and when that permission is granted, privacy and confidentiality should always be upheld.

It's not always possible to secure every aspect of your system, and if there was a way of doing that, then very few companies would afford its cost. This perhaps explains why a security expert only attempts to find a balance between usability and security.

Chapter 1 – The Basics of Ethical Hacking

Just like malicious hackers, ethical hackers employ similar techniques to penetrate and bypass a security system's defense line. However, other than take advantage of the system's vulnerability, they document their findings and propose actionable insight into mechanisms of plugging the hole. The chief role of an ethical hacker is to evaluate and establish how secure or vulnerable a system or network infrastructure is. They seek to find out if a malicious activity is possible, if the system is configured poorly, if there's a hardware flaw, software flaw, or any other operational threat. A threat in this case refers to any condition, circumstance, or agent that can potentially harm, damage, or compromise a system's IT asset. When present, such threats hurt a number of system aspects, including confidentiality, availability, and integrity. Direct consequences include destruction of data, modification of data, corruption of data, and unauthorized disclosure.

Common Types of Threats

Yes, your mother might have warned you off strangers a few years ago. She definitely knew how dangerous the world is out there. The same holds in the computer world. Certain software programs can be loaded with bugs to exploit vulnerabilities in your systems. This ultimately leads to unauthorized access to specific system resources only accessed.

Socially-engineered Trojans: Trojans are programs that masquerade as genuine, safe applications when they are actually malicious. As a computer user, you download such applications thinking that they're legitimate programs. Once installed on your machine, these programs log your key strokes with the objective of recording your passwords.

Normally, the website will throw you a popup saying that your machine is infected by some virus, and that it's important that you run some antivirus. When you choose to run the antivirus, a fake program installs on your machine. You may also be told that you're running out of disk space. In this case, the site suggests a fake defrag program. Clicking on it automatically executes the malware. The fake programs may also hijack your webcam, allowing the hacker to watch your moves as you type in your passwords. Socially-engineered Trojans account for the largest percentage of successful hacks today. This threat can however be solved if the end-user is educated on safe Internet surfing. An up-to-date anti-malware program would also help thwart such attacks.

Phishing Threats: This is where some malicious persons under the disguise of trustworthy persons or businesses, attempt to obtain financial information or other sensitive information fraudulently through fake emails or mass messages. These emails may even remind you to be wary of fraudulent emails, while at the same time requesting for sensitive information through rogue links. There are a number of ant-phishing tools out there to help you repulse such attacks.

Hacker attacks: Malicious persons may bypass your system's security layer to steal, alter, or destroy information.

Denial of Service attacks: DoS attacks, as they're often known, largely involve the use of multiple computers to overwhelm a single server, and ultimately shut it down.

Viruses & spyware: A virus refers to a computer program that eats up your disk space by undergoing multiple replications. Usually, a virus will be transferred to another computer via some portable media such as a USB drive or over a network. Spyware on the hand infects your computer through harmful software downloads. They'll install without your permission and execute on their own, and are usually intended to capture user information. Common infection points of spyware include shareware downloads and other forms of peer-to-peer file sharing.

Adware: Adware refers to some rogue software that displays adverts to your computer, usually after installing software obtained free of charge. You may be receiving the free application in exchange for their ads. However, some adware are designed to intrude your privacy and should be neutralized using anti-malware programs.

Rootkit: A rootkit refers to an assortment of tools used by "black hat" hackers to enjoy administrator-level access privileges on your computer or network. A cybercriminal finds vulnerabilities of certain applications already installed on your PC, and exploits such holes to install spyware programs.

Spam: You've definitely been a victim of spamming. Spam is simply unsolicited junk mail. Today, it's estimated that 70% of the emails we receive in a day is spam. Other than overloading mail servers and being extremely annoying, spam significantly eats into your network bandwidth.

Network-travelling worms: Network-travelling worms such as Zeus and Conficker are very common with email attachments. Worms make use of your network to infect other computers. They're self-replicating and self-spreading. To infect other computers on your network, they don't require any user intervention. Because of their self-replicating behavior, worms at up your bandwidth and degrade your network. Worms could also be used to deliver payloads, which allows hackers to illegally access infected computers. When they manage to access these computers, they turn them into "zombies", which can later be used as Botnets to spam computer users or send DDoS attacks.

Ethical hacking, popularly appreciated as penetration testing or intrusion testing, is a variant of information security that comes in handy when neutralizing the aforementioned threats. For instance, any organization that runs a web store should think of keeping a team of ethical hackers.

Chapter 2 – The Anatomy of Password Hacking

Passwords are ubiquitously used the world over for authentication purposes. Username and password combinations are used to gain access to bank accounts, computer systems, information systems, ATMs, and much more. Prior to accessing your system, you'll need a valid user ID (your username) associated with the system, and a verifiable password. A forensic investigator will hack one or two passwords to access to access a suspect's system, email account, or hard drive. Some are cracked easily, while others are difficult and require advanced computer resources to hack or crack.

By and large, passwords are saved as hashes, and not clear text. You've probably seen asterisk as you type your password. Hashes make use of cryptographic functions to "encrypt" every password input, making it hard for hackers to decrypt or recreate it. To hash your passwords, most systems use SHA-3 or MD5. This is important in ensuring integrity in a sense that should someone modify it, you get to know it. Technically, hashing accepts some arbitrary input (numerals, alphabets, characters, or a combination of these) and generates another string with a defined length. The fixed-length string will have a number of attributes. For instance, the same input string will always generate the same output string, and inverting the output to reproduce the input isn't possible. Any slight modification to the input string drastically changes the hash, and no two outputs will have the same output. Hashing is therefore used together with authentication mechanisms to inform if a particular data set has been modified.

You will also discover that during authentication, the system doesn't "decrypt" the saved password; it simply stores the password's one-way hash. When you supply your password to the system, the system runs an algorithm to generate a one-way hash. The generated hash is then compared with what was stored earlier; if there's a match, access is granted.

To hack or crack a password, you'll therefore need a copy of the hash stored on the user's server to generate a matching copy of your own. Only when you have a perfect match of the hash can you be able to log into the system successfully. It's a tedious process and requires automation. These hashes are usually stored in the most secure part of your system to limit hacker access. In Windows, you'll find the hashes within the SAM file, whereas Linux stores its passwords under the etc/shadow file. This information can only be accessed by system administrators with privileges to access the system's root.

Password Hacking Techniques

To hack your account and steal personal information, hackers use different techniques to attack. Some of these methods can be awesomely simple and low-tech, like guessing a password; others such as social engineering are just crude, while some are way sophisticated. Password hacking can be as easy as conning unsuspecting people into sharing their passwords. This password hacking technique is known as social engineering. Regular security training and user awareness is perhaps the best way of counteracting this threat. Other password hacking techniques are reasonably complex and may require sophisticated tools. Common methods of password attack include:

- **Dictionary Attack**

In a dictionary attack, a hacker tries to encrypt a list of words (usually dictionary words), one word after the other, in the hope that the words will encrypt in a fashion similar to that of the one-way hash saved in the system. When there's a matching hash, the dictionary word that was tried is taken as the password, and in this case, the password is said to be cracked. Most dictionary crackers can manipulate words in the dictionary list by adding advanced variations; for example, if your wordlist had the word "iron", the attack attempts other variations such as "IRON", "1ron", "1R0n", and many others. This is done to ensure that all possible permutations of the word are tried to see if they encrypt to the system's hash.

- **Brute Force Attack**

A brute force attack can last an entire week. Wondering how this is possible? Unlike the dictionary cracker, brute force checks every possible password and its combinations until it finds a match. It might be time consuming, but when given sufficient resources (processor and time), brute force will crack every password.

- **Hybrid Attack**

A hybrid attack involves adding numbers and other symbols (special characters) to a possible password. Simply put, it's a combination of brute force and dictionary attacks, where you employ brute force attack on your wordlist. Brute force is applied to every password on the wordlist, one by one, until the right match is obtained. For example, if you have a word like "password" on your dictionary list, a hybrid attack attempts a combination such as "pa$$word123."

- **Rainbow Tables**

It has also become common for hackers to rely on pre-computed lists of hashes and passwords to hack into systems. Now that all possible passwords have already been computed, all the attacker does is to extract the one-way hash and look up the plaintext password in a rainbow table.

- **Password Capturing**

Today, an attacker will easily capture a targeted password simply by loading a Trojan on your system. Through keyboard-sniffing, the Trojan horse is capable of logging keystrokes and stealing your passwords. This is known as password capturing.

- **Password Sniffing**

It's also common for password crackers to sniff and extract password hashes from authentication traffic between unsuspecting clients and the server. They may also extract other authentication information just enough to initiate the hacking process.

Note: A successful password hacking strategy should take advantage of multiple iterations when cracking passwords. First iterations should target the simplest passwords. The most complicated passwords will require more iteration to crack.

- **Garbage Collecting/Dumpster Diving**

Some hackers sift through garbage for passwords, credit card info, memos, diskettes, hard drives, and other sensitive reports to kick start their malicious process.

- **Password Cracking Software & Hardware**

Find here the most commonly used password cracking software and hardware.

Software

- John the Ripper
- Ophcrack
- LophtCrack
- Cain and Abel
- THC-Hydra
- Brutus
- Aircrack-Ng

Hardware

- Botnet
- GPU
- ASIC

Chapter 3 – Cracking Wireless Networks

In a password protected wireless connection, data is sent from one node to another via encrypted packets. Wondering how this data is encrypted? The various packets of data are usually encrypted with your network's security keys. All you need to access such a connection would be the password used to secure the network. The basic forms of encryption for wireless networks are WEP and WPA. Compared to WPA, WEP is more unsafe and vulnerable given the ease with which it can be cracked. The Wireless Alliance came up with WPA and WPA2 security protocols to address the various security challenges encountered with WEP. There's still however a way of bypassing WPA or WPA2 security if you can mess up their WPS. Compared to their wired counterparts, wireless networks are relatively easier to crack.

Ever thought of breaking into a neighbor's house? Walking through the door may be the easiest option, but that doesn't mean that there are no other entry points, in fact better points. Similarly, you can access a secured network differently, and with different results.

What a good way to start than hack into your own network? Find out how to go about it.

Wi-Fi Hacking Techniques

To hack into high security wireless encryption forms like WPA and WPA2, you'll need a couple of things and tools to succeed.

Requirements

1. A built-in Wi-Fi device or an external Wi-Fi adapter

2. Kali Linux Operating system, which comes with Wifite, a wireless auditing tool that automatically attacks wireless networks

Note: For less secure networks like WEP, a plug-and-play wireless USB adapter would be adequate. Personally, I have been using TP-LINK TL-WN722N, which I obtained from Amazon. You'll however fond better hardware depending on your desired range. For better rage, you'll be more comfortable with Alfa AWUSO36NH or TP-LINK TL-ANT2424B 2.4GHz 24dBi than my choice.

Wi-Fi Hacking With Wifite

Wifite is a fully-automated, mass WEP and WPA hacker that runs largely on its own without much of your intervention.

First, you'll want to **view a list of available access points:**

1. Make sure you are using the Linux OS

2. Go to **Application**

3. Find **Kali Linux**, go to **Wireless Attacks, select 802.11 wireless tools,** and go to **Wifite.**

4. If you can't find Wifite, simply run the command **gedit/usr/bin/wifite** to open Wifite. You should now be able to view a list of the various access points available. You'll have to wait for a few seconds to see nearby wireless access points such as WEP or WPA2

As mentioned in an earlier section, it's much easier to hack a WEP key than any other encryption form: WPA or WPA2.

To hack a WEP encryption with Wifite:

1. Type the command **wifite –h** to familiarize yourself with Wifite commands. Use the command **wifite –showb** to see your targets (access points)

2. Type **Ctrl+C** and then choose and enter your target NUM ESSID (1, 2, 3, 4...n) from the list to crack it. Be sure to separate them with commas if they are more than one. Other than selecting target numbers, you can also select "all" to hack all the discovered WEP Wi-Fi networks

3. Wifite automatically starts the cracking process. The process is absolutely easy and straightforward. It should take 10 minutes or less. To exit Wifite, simply press **Ctrl+C** again

4. At the end of the crack process, you'll be presented with the network's WEP key in the session summary. What you'll see is a hexadecimal format of the Wi-Fi's password. You can then use that key in its raw form to access the wireless network or convert it into a human readable form. To convert from hexadecimal representation to plain text, use online **Hex-to-ASCII converters**.

Tips:

Use these commands to crack WEP secured wireless access points:

1. To crack all the discovered access points, use the command **./wifite.py -all – nowpa**

2. To crack access points with 50dB as their signal strength or more than that, use the command **./wifite.py -p 50 –nowpa**

3. To crack the wireless access points endlessly until there's an interrupt from the user, use the command **./wifite.py -e "testnetwork" -wepw 0**

4. To see the entire list if Wifite commands, type the command **./wifite.py – help**

5. To stop the scanning of access points, simply type **Ctrl+C**

Note: WPA is the short form for Wi-Fi Protected Access. WPA2 on the other hand stands for Wi-Fi Protected Access II. WPS is Wi-Fi Protected Setup, while WEP stands for Wired Equivalent Privacy.

WPA Hacking with Handshake

WPA and WPA2 encryptions are a little tougher to crack than their WEP counterpart. The process is however easier if the network's password is shorter (contains few characters) than when the password is longer. Hacking a WPA key requires the handshake technique. You can capture the handshake file by sniffing through authentication traffic between the router and client. In this case, the router refers to the Wi-Fi's access point, while client is the Wi-Fi enabled device (computer, tablet, or smartphone). Wondering why you need the handshake file? The handshake file carries the Wi-Fi's password, though in an encrypted format. Simply put, your handshake file contains the one-way hash discussed in chapter 2. To a large extent, cracking a WPA password entails **catching the handshake** and **cracking its hash**.

To capture the handshake:

It's not possible to capture the handshake if there's no handshake in the first place. You are either going to sit and wait for a client to show up and connect to the network, or simply choose to disconnect a client who's already connected and wait for them to reconnect. You can then catch their handshake as they connect or reconnect to the WPA network.

When Wifite finally captures the handshake, it attempts to crack it using the dictionary list you provided. Brute force is also applied to find every possible password. When Wifite finds the passphrase, it stops and shows it on the screen. Otherwise, Wifite runs through the entire dictionary list until it finds the key.

To hack a WPA encryption with Wifite's Handshake:

1. Issue the command **gedit /usr/bin/wifite** to open Wifite

2. Replace every single occurrence of the command **cmd = ['aireplay-ng'**, with **cmd = ['aireplay-ng','–ignore-negative-one**

3. Type and enter the command **–wpa** to exclusively target WPA secured networks

4. Use the **–dict** command to give Wifite a wordlist file for cracking the passphrase. Use the command **/usr/share/wordlists** to locate your wordlist

5. Wifite will then automatically start to scan for nearby WPA or WPA2 access points

6. Type and enter **Ctrl+C** to specify your target number. Wifite will start sniffing for the handshake. When it finds it, the passphrase cracking process starts automatically

7. When the cracking process is successful, your passphrase will be shown on the screen as the key

Note: To successfully capture the handshake, a client should log onto the network during that time when you're monitoring the WPA or WPA2 network

Tips:

To make your wireless network more secure:

1. Change your Wi-Fi security to WPA/WPA2 if it's a WEP

2. Disable WPS if it's enabled

3. Change your password periodically

4. Always enable the encryption setting of your router. Encryption methods include those mentioned in point (1)

5. Always turn on your router's built-in firewall

6. Change the default passwords that come with your wireless router. This is the first thing you should do when you log into your wireless router for the very first time. To change the value, simply go to the Settings page of your wireless router and change the username and password values from "admin/password" to other unique value.

7. Remember to change your network's default name. Your network's name is usually set to the default SSID, which is the router's brand name. For example, your network's name could be Linksys or any other manufacturer's ID.

8. Turn off the feature that broadcasts your network's name to the public. This feature should only be turned on if you're running a business, library, hotel, or restaurant, and you intend to offer Wi-Fi Internet to your customers. This feature is however redundant for a home Wi-Fi or any other private network.

9. Make use of your router's MAC address filter. Every single device that connects to your Wi-Fi network is usually associated with a unique ID or a physical address, also known as the MAC address. Your wireless router has an inbuilt feature that could scan the physical addresses of any device connecting to it. You can therefore preset you router to accept only specific devices with recognizable MAC addresses.

10. Turn off your wireless network when not in use

11. Have antivirus and antispyware programs installed on computers allowed to access your Wi-Fi

12. Cap the range of your Wi-Fi signal if you're using your network in a confined place. If for example you're using 802.11b, you may want to switch you router's mode to 802.11g.

13. Always check to confirm that you have the latest firmware on your router

14. Make sure that the remote administration feature is disabled. This feature is usually disabled by default, but it won't cost you anything to double check

Chapter 4 –Hacking Windows

Windows interactive logon screen is the system's first phase of user authentication. This interactive logon makes it easier to allow login access only to authorized users. It's however still very possible to crack this password and gain access to the computer system. When you create a new user account, the password that you assign it is usually converted to a hash before it's stored in the SAM file. SAM is the short form for Security Accounts Manager. This database stores all your Windows passwords as LM and NTLM. These are hashed formats of the passwords. When the user logs on, the password he enters is converted to a hash, and then compared to the hash stored in the SAM database. When there's a match, authentication is approved. Otherwise, the user is denied access.

When you already have your Windows running, you cannot move, copy, or open the SAM file. This explains why you always get an error when you attempt to access the SAM file in the "**C:\windows\system32\config**". The contents of this file are also encrypted to ensure that even when you gain access to the file, you cannot see plain text passwords.

How to Crack Your Windows Password

To crack your Windows logon password, you'll need access to the SAM file, and because the file cannot be accessed in an active Windows session, you'll need a live OS or bootable CD. Once we obtain the hashed passwords, cracking the password becomes easier. We can use the Brute force technique as discussed in a previous section to find the right password. Alternatively, now that we have the SAM file and the one-way hash, we can clear it completely and replace with another. This allows us to modify the old password.

Hack into Windows with Ophcrack

Ophcrack gives you full access to every data object the user of the account can access. This includes data and passwords and all other encrypted files on the computer. To crack your Windows password with Ophcrack:

1. Simply download Ophcrack

2. Create a live CD

3. Boot up your computer on it

4. Once it boots, you'll see a desktop interface as Ophcrack attempts to crack the password

5. When it succeeds, passwords will pop up on the interface. If it fails to find the password, you'll also be notified

Chapter 5 – Hacking Websites

Today, almost every single business has a website to cater for its online community. To buy their favorite items on ecommerce sites or web stores, online buyers use forms to share personal information and other credentials with the seller. Usually, forms are used to transfer this data together with user credentials from the client side to the serve side. Web users also store credit card details on their online profiles within their accounts and because this information is very sensitive, it's of the essence that its integrity and availability is protected at all times. Penetration testing is therefore, important to reveal any security loopholes that cybercriminals may exploit to misrepresent online customers and engage in fraudulent activities. Website security is therefore absolutely paramount.

To begin, start by hacking into your own website. This sounds less criminal, doesn't it? There are a number of methods and tools that you can use to hack into a website. The most popular techniques include:

- **SQL Injection**

SQL injection is a form of website attack where an attacker injects malicious pieces of code (SQL commands) into form fields or URLs to illegally access a site's database. This is possible on vulnerable sites with poorly coded forms. Through such entry points, a hacker is able to access other databases hosted on the server or any other server on the network. SQL injections could target logon pages, contact forms, feedback fields, search functions, shopping carts, support requests, and numerous other functions that submit dynamic web content. The aim of the hacker is to receive certain responses from the site's website that will help him understand a few things on database construction, like table names, number of columns, and other specifics. He will then seek to view data in key tables or to add new data to existing tables. For example, he may opt to add a new user account or manipulate the tables in any other way that could be catastrophic to your business or organization.

- **Web Parameter Tampering**

Clients usually exchange certain parameters with the server on a regular basis via a web page form. A malicious user can hijack the process to modify the user's application data, update his shopping list, or change user permissions without authorization. A hacker can tamper with some of the parameters provided by the user either in the web page form or URL. As a result, the user is redirected to unintended link, web page, or site. This kind of web attack is known as parameter tampering attack. This type of attack is common with identity thieves out to steal user information (personal and business related information). Parameter tampering tools include Paros Proxy and Webscarab. To prevent this type of attack, it's important that you always validate user input and check to confirm that service requests are coming from authorized users.

- **Cross-site Scripting Attack (XSS Attack)**

The XSS attack is an injection attack where the attacker sends malicious scripts to another user's browser with the objective of accessing their session tokens, cookies, and other sensitive data that the user's browser retains. Normally, the unsuspecting user will execute the browser-side script assuming it's from a trusted source. There are two major types of XSS attacks: stored XSS and reflected XSS. Stored XSS is where the attacker stores the malicious script on the end-user's server. Reflected XSS on the other hand is where the malicious code is send to the end-user's browser through alternative routes, like via an email message.

- **DDoS Attack**

This method of attack is largely used by attackers out to shut down the victim's website. In this form of attack, multiple systems (often compromised) are targeted at a single system, overwhelming it with illegitimate service requests, and ultimately causing it to shut down. Stopping this attack is usually hard because the victim's system is flooded with traffic from different sources. DDoS attacks use multiple devices and Internet connections, and are often distributed using botnets.

- **Cookie Poisoning**

Cookie poisoning refers to the alteration of cookies with the intention of accessing unauthorized information. The attacker uses such stolen information to access the victim's accounts or to open new ones. Cookies are usually stored on your hard drive with pieces of information that make it easier for the sites you visit to authenticate your ID, streamline your transactions, and to tailor their presentation for you. Unfortunately, unauthorized persons can also these cookies. If security measures are not properly put in place, attackers can examine your cookies and edit them to get specific user information. To prevent cookie poisoning, websites should use encryption to protect cookies.

Conclusion

Hacking could start with this guide, but it doesn't end here. This guideline together with the many tips included in it should be able to get you started on your hacking experiments the easy way.

You will however learn more advanced tips as you transition from one hacking method or tool to another. Pick any of the many hacking methods discussed in this guide and start your penetration testing.

www.ingramcontent.com/pod-product-compliance
Lightning Source LLC
Chambersburg PA
CBHW061100050326
40690CB00012B/2684